# inside

GW01454458

## ABOUT ME

Start off by focusing on who you are, what your personality is like and what is important to you.

Getting started
Getting down to it
Getting it straight

## CHANGES

Reflect on your memories from primary school and consider the changes that secondary school might bring.

Getting it together
Getting it on paper
Getting the gist

## JOURNEY

Make sure you know how you'll be travelling to and from your secondary school.

Getting there

## PLACES & FACES

Record names and important locations in your new school.

Getting around
Getting the lowdown
Getting used to it

## TIMETABLE

Work out what all the jargon on your timetable means, get organised and pack your bag.

Getting organised
Getting the lingo
Getting it under control
Getting it all in

## LEARNING

Work out what to expect with homework and think about how you learn best.

Getting worked up
Getting wise

## UNIFORM

Make sure you've got everything you need.

Getting the idea

## RULES

Consider the rules in your new school and how best to follow them.

Getting in line
Getting done
Getting on with it
Getting clued up

## TEACHERS

Start out on the right foot and with the right reputation.

Getting the message

## 5

Make new friends and deal with bullying.

Getting to know you
Getting on
Getting acquainted
Getting it right
Getting tough
Getting it out
Getting it across

## WORRIES

Get help and support for those little niggles.

Getting it fixed
Getting it sorted
Getting some answers
Getting help

## FUTURE

What might yours be like?
Getting ahead
Getting a helping hand

## FAREWELL

Onwards and upwards!
Hurrah
Farewell messages

# getting started

**me**

**me...**

Name:

Age:

Birthday:

Ambition:

Things I'm good at:

Things I'd like to improve at:

# my best...

**Food:**

**Book:**

**Friend:**

**Music:**

**Hobby:**

**Subject:**

**note** 😣 Have a go at filling in the boxes to record all about you!

# my worst...

**Nightmare:**

**Memory:**

**Phobia:**

**Subject:**

**Food:**

**Habit:**

**stuff**

How I'm feeling about starting secondary school:

# getting down to it

**Discuss your responses with a friend or adult.**

|  | yep | sort of | nope |
|---|---|---|---|
| **myself** | | | |
| Can you give three reasons why it's good to be you? | ☐ | ☐ | ☐ |
| Can you state something that you are good at and explain why? | ☐ | ☐ | ☐ |
| Can you state something that you are not so good at and explain why? | ☐ | ☐ | ☐ |
| **classroom** | | | |
| Can you describe (or show) how you'd let your teacher know you are listening? | ☐ | ☐ | ☐ |
| Can you think of three school rules and say why each one is important? | ☐ | ☐ | ☐ |
| Can you talk about something you have learnt this week? | ☐ | ☐ | ☐ |
| **friends** | | | |
| Can you give two reasons why you are a good friend and one thing that would make you an even better friend? | ☐ | ☐ | ☐ |
| Can you describe what you would do if your friend was crying and explain why? | ☐ | ☐ | ☐ |
| Can you suggest two things that you could do if you were being teased? | ☐ | ☐ | ☐ |

|  | yep | sort of | nope |
|---|---|---|---|

**feelings**

Can you name three different feelings and discuss when you have felt them?

Can you explain how you could tell that someone else was feeling sad?

Can you give two ways that might help calm you down if you were feeling angry?

**solving**

Can you explain what you could do if you got stuck on your homework?

Can you suggest two things you might do if you and a friend couldn't agree which game to play?

Can you explain what you would do if you couldn't find your P.E. kit?

**attitude**

Can you think of three reasons why you should come to school?

Can you explain what you would do if you thought your friend was wrong?

Can you state one school rule you agree with and why and one you would change and why?

# getting it straight

**What do you think about school right now?**

What I like best
about school:

What I like least
about school:

I learn best when:

I'm bored when:

I come to school for:

School would be better if:

As Head Teacher, I would:

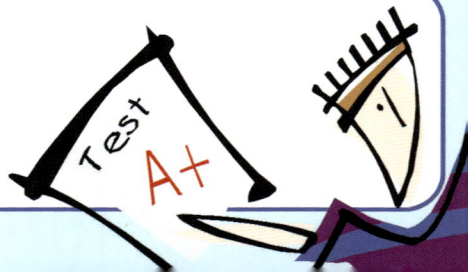

Test
A+

# getting it together

**How do you feel about leaving primary school?**
**Make a note of your memories here.**

Best friends:

Favourite subject:

Greatest achievement:

Inspiring teacher:

Funniest thing:

Most embarrassing thing:

A difficulty I overcame:

Best trip/visit:

Something else I want to remember:

# getting it on paper

**Make sure you have all the information you need.**

My new school:

Form and teacher:

School address:

School telephone number:

School start and finish times:

Where can/did you find this information?

# getting the gist

**Decide where these tags belong in this diagram.
Can you think of any more?**

just at primary

just at secondary

at both primary and secondary

| Bullying | Refectory/Canteen | Tutor Period |
| Just One Classroom | Head Of Year | Homework |
| Foreign Language | Physics | Protractor |

# getting there

## How will you get to your new school?

**BUS**

Get on:

Get off:

Fare price:

Bus number:

Journey time:

Leave at:

Route:

**FOOT**

Walking with:

Journey time:

Leave at:

**CAR**

Driver:

Drop off point:

Journey time:

Leave at:

Route:

**BIKE**

Where to store safely:

Journey time:

Leave at:

What time will you have to get up?

# getting around

## Are you worried about getting lost?

**Tick off these important locations once you've found them around your new school.**

**Write yourself a little clue that will remind you how to find this location again in future.**

- [ ] Student entrance
- [ ] Place to eat lunch
- [ ] Toilets
- [ ] School office
- [ ] Your form room
- [ ] Hall
- [ ] ICT Suite

What other locations are important for you in your new school?

- [ ]
- [ ]
- [ ]

What can you do if you get lost?

# getting the lowdown

**Find out what your school wants you to remember.**
**The first one is just an example.**

| What? | Where? | When? |
|---|---|---|
| To collect a Meal Card for the canteen. | From Mr. Smith's office (Room B10) upstairs in the main building. | At break time on Mondays, Wednesdays or Fridays only. |
| | | |
| | | |
| | | |

# getting used to it

**Who's who in your new school?**
**Find out some names of your teachers,**
**and other VIPs in school.**

| Name? | Who are they? | Funny Fact? |
|---|---|---|
|  |  |  |
|  |  |  |
|  |  |  |
|  |  |  |
|  |  |  |

What are your first impressions of your form tutor?

What do you think your form tutor's first impressions of you are?

# getting organised

## How organised are you?

In the morning before school, you wake up to:

- ★ the sound of your alarm clock which you set the night before
- ★ the sound of your family getting up- it's usually about the right time
- ★ your mum yelling at you to get up or else you'll be late again

Your first lesson of the day is PE. You:

- ★ get changed quickly and start warming up
- ★ change into your stinky kit which hasn't been washed for a while
- ★ have to sit and watch because you forgot your kit

You are a member of a lunchtime club. You:

- ★ check your watch and turn up five minutes early
- ★ wait for midday supervisors to remind you and turn up just in time
- ★ were too busy with your mates, you missed the club altogether

You have some homework to complete. You:

- ★ write it in your homework diary, do it and hand it in on time
- ★ write it on scrap paper, do it, then hand it in a day late
- ★ forget to write it down, forget to do it, forget to hand it in

You've been invited to a party. You:

- ★ turn up on time together with a present and card
- ★ call your friend to check where it is because you lost the invitation
- ★ forget

★ **Mostly Blue**
Super organised!
You're usually on time
and in the right place!
Well done!

★ **Mostly Orange**
Need to improve!
Write a 'To Do' list then
decide which jobs are most
important and do them first!

★ **Mostly Purple**
Disorganised!
Use a diary and a watch!
Tidy up your desk/room/bag so
you know where things are!

# getting the lingo

**Do you know what these acronyms and abbreviations mean?**

PSHE

PBL

RE

MFL

Phys

Bio

D&T

Hums

Chem

VLE

ICT

Hist

Geog

Does your school use any others? Check your timetable!

# getting it under control

**Write down which subjects you have on each day!**

**Write down what you will need on each day!**

| Monday | |
|---|---|
| | |

| Tuesday | |
|---|---|
| | |

| Wednesday | |
|---|---|
| | |

| Thursday | |
|---|---|
| | |

| Friday | |
|---|---|
| | |

Use this chart as a reminder when packing your bag (the night before)!

**Some schools have a 2-week timetable to fit in every subject!**

**Record Week 2.**

| Write down which subjects you have on each day! | Write down what you will need on each day! |
| --- | --- |
| Monday | |
| Tuesday | |
| Wednesday | |
| Thursday | |
| Friday | |

How will you remember whether it's Week 1 or Week 2?

# getting it all in

**Be prepared to get organised!**
**What might these people need to pack in their bags?**

**Preston's Bag**

School
day trip
to the
seaside

Preston might need:

**Jo's Bag**

Shopping
in town
with her
sister

Jo might need:

**Sean's Bag**

His
dad's
house
overnight

Sean might need:

Discuss what you'd need to pack for a day like this...

| W1 | P1 | P2 | P3 | P4 | P5 | P6 |
|------|-------|------|----|------|-----|-----|
| TUES | MATHS | CHEM | PE | HIST | ART | FRE |

## Rita's Bag

Camping for a weekend

Rita might need:

## Joey's Bag

The park with friends

Joey might need:

## Your Bag

Going to school... what items will you need every day?

# getting worked up

**Think about your homework!**

| Which subjects do you get given on which day? | When do you have to hand it in? | On which day will you do this homework? |
|---|---|---|
| Monday | | |
| Tuesday | | |
| Wednesday | | |
| Thursday | | |
| Friday | | |

Leaving homework until the last minute can make you feel stressed which means you're more likely to make mistakes!

'Take five' if you need to re-energise!

Reward yourself when it's done!

Work in a quiet, tidy, comfy space!

Cheating by copying someone else's homework won't help you improve!

Does your school have a homework club you could try out?

## Have a 2-week timetable?  Record Week 2 here!

| Which subjects do you get given on which day? | When do you have to hand it in? | On which day will you do this homework? |
| --- | --- | --- |
| Monday | | |
| Tuesday | | |
| Wednesday | | |
| Thursday | | |
| Friday | | |

Who can you ask for help with your homework?

What would happen if you didn't do your homework?

# getting wise

**Try this quiz to discover your preferred learning style!**

## 1. In a lesson, I prefer the teacher to:

Do a demonstration

Write or draw on the board

Talk about the subject

## 2. I follow instructions best when:

Someone tells me

Someone shows me

They are written

## 3. In my spare time, I enjoy:

Watching TV

Listening to music

Playing a game

## 4. After meeting someone, I am most likely to remember:

What they were doing

What they looked like

What they were saying

## 5. If I could choose, I'd rather take part in:

A Music lesson

An Art lesson

A P.E. lesson

## 6. I most enjoy stories when:

I act it out

Someone reads it aloud

I read it myself

**Mostly** A 'visual learner' likes to observe and see things written or printed in books or on the board. This learner likes colour, lists, charts and diagrams.

**SEE** TIP: Make sure you can see the board.

**Mostly** An 'auditory learner' likes listening, enjoys discussions and talking things through and remembers verbal instructions best.

**HEAR** TIP: Ask questions if you need to.

**Mostly** A 'kinaesthetic learner' likes to be active, use their hands, go exploring, try things out and can put things together easily.

**DO** TIP: Make use of equipment.

UNIFORM

# getting the idea

**What do you think of your new school uniform?**

What do you think of the uniform?

Do you think students should or shouldn't wear uniform? Why?

Where will you get your new uniform from?

What rules about uniform are there in your new school?

Which uniform items do you need? Don't forget PE!

In which jobs would you be required to wear a uniform?

# getting in line

**Pretend that you are the new Head Teacher and imagine that you are changing the rules in your school!**

Which rules do you agree with?

Rule:

Why?

Rule:

Why?

Rule:

Why?

## Which rules do you disagree with?

Rule:

Why?

Rule:

Why?

## Which rules would you add?

Rule:

Why?

Rule:

Why?

# getting done

## If you broke these rules, what consequences would you face at your school?

Being late:

Bullying in the playground:

Talking when you shouldn't be:

Not using the crossing patrol to cross the road:

Do you think these punishments are fair?

Chewing gum in class:

Not doing or not handing in your homework:

Copying someone else's work:

Not playing by the rules in a game:

Stealing:

Why do you think we need rules and punishments?

# getting on with it

**Here are some other kinds of rules for secondary school success!**

Make friends! Join a school club which interests you. It's easier to make friends when you have stuff in common.

Don't put up with bullying. Always tell an adult, even if it isn't you who is being bullied.

Don't panic if your homework is too difficult. Ask someone at home for some help and let your teacher know you found it a bit tricky. Teachers are there to support your learning and won't be cross if you are honest and need to ask them for help.

Keep your school diary or planner up to date so you'll always know what to expect and can be prepared.

Make sure you keep your valuables safe, either in a locker or at home!

What tips have you received from other people?

# getting clued up

RULES

**Have a go at this puzzle to get to grips with some new words!**

## across

1. The meeting place where hot food is served.

3. Another word for a 'mark' for a piece of work.

4. An abbreviation for a subject that explores personal skills.

5. An abbreviation for the teacher in charge of the whole year group.

## down

2. This is another word for your registration group.

4. You might hear someone use this word to mean a lesson.

6. A V.I.P in school that shares a name with a body part.

# getting the message

What would you like your new teacher to know about you? Use this space to introduce yourself!

# getting to know you

**What ingredients would you put into a recipe for friendship?**

good listener

# getting on

**What kind of friend are you?
Try this quiz for fun to find out!**

Which one of these words best describes you?

Outgoing  Reliable  Independent

Do you have a big group of friends?  Do you have one or two close friends?  Do you prefer your own company?

Y  N  Y  N  N  Y

Do your friends have similar interests?  N  Do you often try to make people laugh?  N  Do your friends often hang around with others?  N  Do your friends share their secrets with you?  N

Y  Y  Y  Y

Do you usually stick with same group?  N  Do you enjoy working in a team?  Can you easily start a conversation with someone?  Is it important to you to have friends?  N  Do you prefer doing things on your own?

Y  Y  N  Y  N  Y  N  Y

## Busy Bee

You probably have a big crowd of friends who you tend to stick with. You're a real team player and are great at sharing and joining in.

For making a best friend, try finding out who is the most similar to you.

## Social Butterfly

You have lots of friends but float around, choosing different friends each day. You are sociable and try hard to please others but are not sure who to trust.

For friends who are always there, try joining a team at your school.

## Faithful Hound

You are likely to have a few carefully selected close friends. You're reliable and trustworthy but perhaps can be shy around new people.

To feel confident around new people, try inviting just one new person to join in a game with your friends.

## Solitary Sole

You are independent and enjoy your own company. You probably don't like team games and can be nervous around other people.

To meet new friends with similar interests, try joining a school club or team!

# getting acquainted

## See what you can find out about your new classmates!

Write down the name of someone who...

...travels to school in the same way as you:

...shares the same favourite subject as you:

...plays a musical instrument:

...speaks another language:

...has a different hobby to you:

What would life be like if everyone was exactly the same?

# getting it right

## What might these **friends** be saying?

Name two people who
are good friends to you:

Are you a good
friend to them?

# getting tough

## ...and what might these **bullies** be saying?

**Bullying is wrong. Name two adults you could speak to if you or someone you know is being bullied:**

# getting it out

## What could you say to join in the conversation?

That film was rubbish! Waste of money!

Yeah. Wish we'd seen the other film!

I really liked the very end bit though!

Hope the neighbours don't complain about the loud music!

It's a great disco though! Look. I bought this new T-shirt to wear!

## Top Tips!

**Make eye contact!**
This helps the person feel you are paying attention to them. Try not to stare though!

**Listen!**
Give the person time to speak and nod to show you've heard.

**Ask a question!**
Make it relevant and not too personal. This shows the person you're interested in what they are saying.

**Say something nice!**
Paying someone a compliment helps them to feel good about themselves and about talking to you!

**Smile! It's relaxing!**

How was your holiday? Did you have a good time?

Hey, bet it was hot, you look like you've got a bit of a tan!

Great, thanks! The best bit was playing in the pool with my sister!

How about holding a debate?

**A debate is when people discuss both sides of an argument. Speaking and listening skills are very important in a debate.**

**Try these topics to get you started!**

It should be made illegal to ride a bike without a helmet.

Under 12's should not be allowed a TV in their bedroom.

Mobile phones should not be allowed in schools.

School uniform is uneccessary and should be banned.

**Practice speaking and listening!** Some people find it difficult to know what to talk about. These topics can be useful but remember it takes two people to have a conversation so don't just talk about yourself, ask questions too.

What you will be doing at the weekend

How you found the homework

What you enjoyed watching on TV

What you want to be when you're older

**What other topics can make good conversations?**

# getting it across

**Things aren't always as straight forward as they first seem.
What do you think about these scenarios?**

## Jordan

overhears a gang saying something nasty about his best mate. He tells his best mate what the boys were saying about him because he thinks he should know.

**Jordan should tell his best mate what was said.**

| Strongly Agree | Agree | Not Sure | Disagree | Strongly Disagree |

Why?

## Becky

buys a magazine at the shop and pays at the counter. The shop assistant gives her too much change. She decides not to tell him and keep the extra money.

**Becky shouldn't admit to the extra change.**

| Strongly Agree | Agree | Not Sure | Disagree | Strongly Disagree |

Why?

## Joshua

is being forced by some older kids to do something he doesn't want to do. He decides to do it because he doesn't want to get beaten up.

**Joshua should do as the older kids tell him.**

| Strongly Agree | Agree | Not Sure | Disagree | Strongly Disagree |

Why?

## Sandeep

really wants to buy a birthday present for her mum as a special surprise. She lies about where she is going so that she can keep it a secret.

### Sandeep should lie.

| Strongly Agree | Agree | Not Sure | Disagree | Strongly Disagree |
|---|---|---|---|---|

Why?

## Chelsea

thinks her best friend's new hair cut is unflattering and untrendy. She doesn't want to tell a lie so she tells her best friend what she truly thinks.

### Chelsea should tell her friend the truth.

| Strongly Agree | Agree | Not Sure | Disagree | Strongly Disagree |
|---|---|---|---|---|

Why?

## Lee

is worried about a friend who told him a secret and begged him not to tell. Lee thinks his friend may be in danger but he doesn't tell a soul.

### Lee should keep quiet.

| Strongly Agree | Agree | Not Sure | Disagree | Strongly Disagree |
|---|---|---|---|---|

Why?

Write about a time when you had to make a hard decision...

# getting it fixed

## What advice can you give the people below?

I'm worried about what my mum will say when she finds out I got a detention today.

DETENTION

I'm worried about what it will be like at lunchtime when I go to secondary school.

LUNCH ROOM

**Whose advice do you trust? Why?**

# getting it sorted

What are you worried about or really want to know about your new secondary school? Write it down then list three different things you could do to alleviate the problem or find an answer! Which path will you choose?

So. what's up?

1

2

3

# getting some answers

## Some things you might feel too afraid to ask...

I'm worried because I don't know anyone going to my secondary school. How will I make friends?

Don't panic! This happens to lots of people so there will probably be others worrying about trying to make new friends too!

Schools often have an Induction Day which is where they invite new students to come and meet other people who will be in their class. Ask your Year 6 teacher about this. There will usually be lots of activities on the first day as well, just to help you get to know everyone. Learning new names can take a while but try to always smile and say hello as this can make people feel relaxed and want to be your friend.

Try joining a school club so you can mix with others who enjoy the same hobbies as you and that's always a good start because you will know what to talk about!

Can you get home another way? Be sure to check at home first and let the school know of your change of plans.

If you absolutely have to get the bus home, maybe you could team up with a friend? Sometimes, it just feels safer to be with other people you know. Perhaps you could even get to know some older pupils at your school by joining a school club, most of them aren't as bad as you think! If the nasty comments happen again, let an adult in school know; they may help contact the bus company. Remember, bullying is wrong and must be dealt with.

Don't make the mistake of waiting until the last minute to run to the bus stop as you might miss your ride home!

I get the bus home from school and there are loads of year 11s who are loud and noisy and shove everyone around. I don't like it. One girl even took the mick out of me.

Yeah, the canteen/refectory/dining hall can get very hectic at lunchtime! Some schools try to calm this by having a rota system to allocate each year group a time to get their lunch. If not, head there with a friend so you can queue together and not feel so lost amongst the crowd. Or else, you could try bringing in a packed lunch of course!

If your school has Meal Cards, they will tell you how to use them. Usually, it's a bit like credit for 'pay as you go' mobile phones where you pay some money onto a card. This prevents you from losing money or having money stolen from you, as only you can use your Meal Card.

*What am I meant to do at lunchtime? The canteen looked so busy on my induction day. What are meal cards?*

*There's a girl in my class who smells horrible, especially after P.E. I feel sorry for her because there's a group of girls who bully her but I don't think she realises it's because she has B.O. What should I do?*

Imagine how this poor girl feels! Well done for not joining in with these girls! That is tough for some people because they join in to avoid being picked on by the gang themselves! By not helping you're a 'bystander' which means that you let the bullying carry on. That can be just as bad!

Tell an adult! They won't have to tell anyone that it was you who told, so don't worry about being called a 'grass', 'snitch' or anything else! Perhaps you could make friends with the girl; she might be feeling very lonely. Maybe once you've gained her trust, you could talk to her in a kind way – you could talk about your favourite perfumes, or suggest she might want to try out your new body spray. If you feel confident, chat to the gang about this girl and stick up for her a bit. They might not realise how they are hurting her.

All schools have a policy on uniform explaining all their rules about what you can and can't wear. Sometimes, this is for Health & Safety reasons, to prevent accidents happening, like in P.E. for example. Religious items are usually allowed but have a chat to your form tutor at school who will be able to check. Ask a parent to write a letter so that your school is aware of your beliefs.

*I have to wear certain things because of my religious faith. I've heard that my school bans jewellery. How can I get this sorted?*

# farewell messages

**Ask your friends and teachers to write either their Year 6 farewell or Year 7 welcome messages of support!**

## Check List

**Make sure you can tick these vitals off as soon as possible!**

**Yes**

Do you know your form tutor's name?
Can you name three new classmates?
Do you know where the toilets are?
Do you have lunchtime food arrangements?
Do you have transport arrangements?
Have you discussed any worries with an adult?